This
Book
Belongs
To _

Grolier Enterprises Inc.
SHERMAN TURNPIKE, DANBURY, CONNECTICUT 06816

Book Club Edition

The STORY Of BABY JESUS

Written by Alice Joyce Davidson
Illustrated by Victoria Marshall

Text copyright ©1985 by Alice Joyce Davidson
Art copyright ©1985 by The C.R. Gibson Company
Published by The C.R. Gibson Company
Norwalk, Connecticut 06856
Printed in the United States of America
All rights reserved
ISBN 0-8378-5072-X
D.L. TO: 204-1988

A little girl named Alice
Was as busy as can be;
She helped make decorations
For a big tall Christmas tree.

On Christmas Eve she went to church,
Wrapped gifts for everyone,
Then picked up her Bible storybook
When all her work was done.

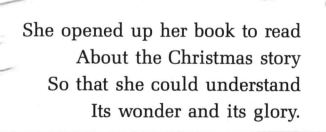

She opened up her book to read
About the Christmas story
So that she could understand
Its wonder and its glory.

On a slightly open window,
Alice heard a rap-tap-tap;
The airmail bird flew in and
Left this letter on her lap:
"Reading is the magic key
To take you where you want to be."

The Bible storybook became
A great big open screen;
Alice walked on through to Bibleland
And came upon this scene.

She saw a woman, Mary,
Whose face was very fair,
Nearing Bethlehem with Joseph
To pay a great tax there.

Mary was going to have a baby,
Perhaps that very night,
But Bethlehem was crowded,
With not a room in sight.

Mary looked so tired,
That an innkeeper felt pity
And offered them his stable,
The last room in the city.

Not far away some shepherds,
Looked in fear up at the skies;
They saw an angel coming down,
His bright light filled their eyes.

"Don't be afraid," the angel said,
"For I bring you news of joy.
Tonight in Bethlehem was born
A holy baby Boy!"

"He's Christ, the Lord, a Savior!
He'll save people everywhere!
He's sleeping in a manger.
You'll find Him lying there!"

Suddenly the angel
Was joined by many more.
The angels sang a song of praise
To God whom they adore.

"Glory to our Father,
To God who reigns above,
Peace on earth, good will to all,
God sends His gift of love."

The angels finished singing
Their praise-filled song, and then
They rose up through the star-filled skies
To heaven once again.

"Let's hurry on to Bethlehem!"
The shepherds cried with joy.
They hastened through the starry night
To see this holy Boy.

When the shepherds reached the stable,
They saw a wondrous sight,
For Mary's little Baby
Had been born that very night.

There in that humble stable,
Among the oxen and the sheep,
As His mother watched in wonder,
The Son of God lay fast asleep.

The shepherds knelt in wonder
To see this miracle of birth.
It was as the angel told them;
God had sent His love to earth.

Mary called her baby "Jesus"
And with a mother's tender touch,
She wrapped a little blanket
'Round this child she loved so much.

The shepherds spread the joyous news
About the Savior's birth
And how this child would change the world
By bringing love to earth.

Now in the East a bright new star
Shone both night and morn;
Three wise men who had seen the star
Knew a King was born.

They wanted to adore Him
So traveled from afar.
They knew that they would find the King
By following the star.

The star brought them to Bethlehem;
It stopped above the door.
Inside they found the Baby
They had wanted to adore.

The wise men fell upon their knees
Before the newborn King,
And being there with Jesus
Caused their happy hearts to sing.

The men gave Jesus special gifts,
Then stood up to depart,
And all these things that happened
Mary treasured in her heart.

Now the time had come for Alice
To walk back through her screen.
She tiptoed home from Bibleland
And thought of what she'd seen.

Alice thought about the shepherds
And the star that shone above;
She thought about the wise men
And God's wondrous gift of love.

Alice thought about the newborn King
And the angels' song of glory
And found she knew the meaning
Of the wondrous Christmas story.

On Christmas morn when Alice woke,
She raced down to the tree,
And sang this special song of praise
For all her family.

"Glory to our God on high,
Glory to our King!
Praise Him like the angels,
Let our happy voices ring!"

"Glory to our God above
Who so loved everyone,
He gave the world a gift of love—
Jesus Christ, His Son!"

"Glory to our God of love
This joyous Christmas morn
And Happy Birthday, Jesus,
On this day that You were born!"